GUYLO

By Mindy Drayer

ISBN: 978-1-62249-507-8

Published by
Biblio Publishing
Columbus, Ohio
BiblioPublishing.com

Contents

Chapter 1

THE ONE

There he was. In the corner of the pen surrounded by his littermates. For some reason, I was immediately drawn to this adorable, dark colored puppy with oversized ears. I noticed him right away and he noticed me. His eyes locked with mine as he tilted his head and let out a barely noticeable whimper. He seemed to be making a decision about me as well. Without hesitation, I knew in my heart he was the one. I picked him up and a warm sensation filled my entire body. My heart melted and I didn't want to let go. Just like that, I found what I was looking for.

Most people have their favorite breed of dogs. They choose that breed because of appearance, personality or personal experience. I have always loved German Shepherds. My passion for that specific breed developed when I was a young girl. There used to be a 1970's television show called Run Joe Run. It was about a German Shepherd named Joe that escaped from an army base. The dog was wrongfully accused of attacking his trainer and was supposed to be destroyed as punishment. Joe ran away from the base and met up with a man who befriended the dog. Together, the two traveled through various towns helping people they met along the way.

I loved that show and watched it whenever I could. Joe was so kind, smart, and strong. He was absolutely beautiful. I knew one day that I would have a German

1

Shepherd of my own. That day had finally come, and I couldn't wait!

Fortunately for me, my sister Molly had a friend named Jerry who raised and trained German Shepherds for various law enforcement agencies around the country. Some of the dogs were also sold to everyday people as devoted house pets. Because they were in such high demand, Jerry often had litters of puppies on his property.

There happened to be a family of pups ready for purchase. The timing couldn't have been better. In a few days, I was moving away from home. I was heading to the northwest region of Ohio for my new job. But, I didn't want to go alone. I figured a German Shepherd pup would be the perfect roommate. So, it was time for a road trip. Hopefully I'd return with a new bundle of fur.

Molly and I jumped in my car to pay a visit to her friend Jerry. My anticipation and excitement kept building as I drove to the location of the property. Finally, we arrived. It was a warm summer day and the sun was shining brightly. Jerry walked patiently to the car to greet us. He explained that his German Shepherds were working dogs that could handle heavy training and important responsibilities. Basically, his dogs needed jobs. I thought that was great, but I wondered if they could also handle hugs, kisses, and a lot of love and affection. The pup that I would choose was destined to get all that and more. I was so ready to be a dog mom!

We got out of my car and walked inside a long rectangular building. It was the kennel where the puppies were kept until they got old enough to train or to be purchased as pets.

That's where I found him. From that moment on, I was never alone. I told Jerry that I made my choice. He took the puppy out of my arms and looked him over.

He then handed the friendly pup back to me and said "you picked an outstanding dog. He will grow to be strong, reliable and very protective." Jerry also reminded me to keep him busy by giving him certain jobs to do. Games like fetch and hide and seek would be fine. Dogs consider that work and German Shepherds love to work.

I hopped in my car with the best feeling in the world. My new friend snuggled comfortably in my lap the entire ride home. For the first time in my life, I had my very own puppy.

My family had pets before, dogs, cats, guinea pigs, parakeets, chickens, gerbils, and hermit crabs. But there is something so special about getting your very first dog that belongs to you and you alone.

The next challenge was picking out a name. For those of you who have had dogs, you know how important this part of the process can be. Some dogs are named after significant people or places. Others are based on the color or texture of the animal's coat. The name I came up with had no significant meaning. In fact, I had never heard it before and never heard it again on any other dog or family pet. It came to me quite easily. I kept looking at my new found friend saying "hi little guy." I took the word guy and added the first two letters of love. I guess you could say the name I chose was one of a kind. Guylo...the name fit perfectly. Throughout our time together, Guylo would prove over and over, he truly was one of a kind. Our adventure was about to begin.

Chapter 2.

ON MY OWN

Remember when you moved away from home for the very first time? For many of you, that moment most likely came when you went to college. You got to experience moving into a dorm, meeting new friends, and eating cafeteria food on a regular basis. You also learned what life was like living with people other than family and having to adjust your lifestyle to theirs. Sometimes, that obstacle was harder than it had to be.

You also gained independence with a new sense of freedom. It was now up to you to make wise personal choices that could affect your well-being. Everything from choosing the right (or wrong) people to hang out with, what to eat and drink, when to sleep, where to sleep, and even what to wear. At times, you even forced yourself to study without mom or dad telling you to do so. It was a whole new world of trial and error. And, YOU were the person in charge!

That, however, wasn't the case for me. I attended The Ohio State University in Columbus, Ohio. Because I lived in a suburb nearby, I commuted. So, while all my friends were going off to college and gaining their much-anticipated independence, I stayed at home and continued to live with my parents. I know, I know, it doesn't sound very exciting. But I actually didn't mind commuting. I spent many nights sleeping at my friends' dorms after staying out late, dancing and bar hopping with my friends. I actually preferred college life that way. I could stay on campus when I

4

wanted but could always go back to the quiet and comfort of home. It was kind of like having the best of both worlds.

I did eventually move out on my own though. That unsettling time in my life came several years later than many of you. Instead of cutting the strings after high school graduation, my time for flight came after my fun filled years at Ohio State. It was time to find a job and start a new life away from everything that was familiar to me.

It was the summer of 1992. I was 24 years old and I was ready to explore the world, or at least Ohio. You see, I'm extremely close to my family and friends. I always have been. I never had plans to venture too far from where I grew up (Westerville, Ohio). I have lived in Westerville most of my life. It's a city with a population of nearly 40,000 and sits about 20 miles Northeast of Columbus. It's an absolutely perfect place to raise a family. I know that firsthand. One, from growing up there and two, from raising my own children in Westerville.

Like many of you, I wasn't sure what I wanted to be when I was young. There were several professions that interested me. I thought about becoming a teacher and a coach. In fact, I spent quite a bit of time volunteering as a Sunday school teacher at my church, I also was a little league softball coach and a cheerleading advisor at my old high school Westerville North. I realized that I could always work with kids in some way or another but that I didn't have to make a career out of it.

Another option, becoming a veterinarian. I have always had a life-long passion for animals. It didn't

5

matter if it was a dog or a frog, I always wanted to save, rescue and adopt as many animals as I could. Boy, is that the truth. When I was growing up in our family home on Debbie Drive, my sister Molly and I snuck in chickens, frogs, toads, turtles, birds and snakes. Yes, snakes! Once, we even hid a puppy in our bedroom closet. I can remember, as clear as day, my mom bringing clothes up from the basement and hanging them in our closet while the puppy was inside it. We didn't breathe. We just stood motionless hoping that pup would stay in there without making a sound. It did exactly that. Thank goodness!

But, when it came to making a career out of veterinary medicine, I couldn't do it. I thought it would be too heart-breaking seeing sick or injured animals every single day. What if I couldn't save or help them? That would kill me. Plus, I didn't think I was smart enough for all the medical classes I would have to take.

So, instead of concentrating on the things I couldn't do, I started to focus on what I could do. That was easy because I knew there was always one particular skill I seemed to master at a very early age...talking! I could talk to anyone, at any time. I was never shy and always loved meeting new people. Halfway through college, I figured it out. I wanted to be a TV news reporter and possibly an anchor.

TV broadcasting is an extremely competitive field. It always has been. But, I was willing to give it a try. Fortunately, a friend of mine knew the owners of a small cable TV station/AM radio station in Delaware, Ohio (WDLR). They were looking for a morning radio news anchor and TV reporter. It sounded like the perfect opportunity and I took the job almost immediately after graduating from Ohio State.

It was a fun job and I learned a lot about the business. I even had my own talk show! It was called "Access" With Mindy Drayer. I worked at WDLR a little more than a year. But, I knew I couldn't do this forever. I needed more of a challenge. I really wanted to land a job at an affiliate in Ohio. It didn't matter if it was ABC, CBS, or NBC. But what did matter, was staying relatively close to home.

One day, while researching various job openings, I came across, what seemed to be, an outstanding opportunity at WLIO. It's a small market TV station in Lima, Ohio. Television news stations are assigned a market number. The lower the number, the bigger the city.

For example, there are 210 markets in the United States of America. The number one market is New York City with Los Angeles in second and Chicago third. Lima is market size 190. WLIO is an NBC affiliate about 90 minutes from Westerville. It was perfect. Now, all I had to do was get the job. And, just in case you're wondering ...the smallest market in the United States of America is Glendive, Montana.

While working in Delaware, I really did gain some good experience. I became friends with very powerful people throughout the county like judges, detectives, police officers, politicians and other community leaders. Because of these friendships and the trust I gained along the way, I was often granted exclusive interviews and given choice opportunities like riding along with sheriff's deputies as they conducted undercover sting operations.

One experience after another allowed me to put together a pretty good resume tape of all the exciting stories I covered. I also included a sample of anchoring an evening newscast. After some fancy editing, I was happy with how my tape turned out. The question was, would the news director in Lima like it enough to offer me a job? I was about to find out.

Instead of just sending my resume tape in the mail, I wanted to personally deliver it and try my hardest to get in the door of the newsroom for a face to face meeting. Life is all about taking chances. So, I needed to do just that. But, I wasn't about to do it alone. My mom made the road trip with me. Throughout my entire life, my mom has always been there for me. Her career was taking care of her children. We didn't fully appreciate it while growing up but as my siblings and I grew older, we realized the importance of being a stay at home mom. There truly is nothing more important. Anyway, my mom and I hopped in my car and started heading toward Allen County.

My plan worked like a charm. My mom and I pulled into the parking lot of WLIO. She waited in the car while I walked through the doors of the one-story brick building which looked a lot more like a house than a TV station. I asked if the news director was in. He was, and he actually had a free moment.

His name was George Dunster. He was a charming older man with a serious yet friendly personality. We had a great conversation about my goals and experience. I gave him my resume tape and hoped for the best.

A few days later, I was hired and thrilled! I couldn't believe things were working out so well and so quickly. I also came to the realization that I was about to leave the house I called home for nearly all my life.

I've always had my parents to take care of me and older siblings to look after me. I also had lifelong friends who stayed by my side through every obstacle that came my way. But, that was all about to change. For the first time in my life, I was going out on my own. I needed something. Something that I could take with me, be a part of me. However, I had no idea how that "something" was going to change my life forever.

That was the only reason I drove to Jerry's property on that warm summer day; to find Guylo. He was my something that eventually turned into my everything.

Chapter 3.

THE DEFINING MOMENT

The next major car ride came two days later. I packed up everything I needed for my move to Northwest Ohio. It seemed so strange to be moving away from Westerville. Saying goodbye to family and friends was undeniably painful. Sometimes in life, it's so easy to live in a comfort zone where we are familiar with everything around us. The people and places of Central Ohio were like second nature to me. But, it was time for a change, time to break out of that comfort zone. On the positive side, I wasn't going to experience this change alone. I had Guylo and within those first few days together, we immediately grew attached to one another. Right from the very beginning and without hesitation, Guylo clumsily followed me all around my parents' house and yard or wherever we went. He never let me walk alone. I had an instant shadow. I just had no idea how much I would depend on that shadow.

After one final and tearful embrace with my parents, we were ready to make the trip away from home. I can't tell you how difficult it was to say goodbye to my mom and dad. They've always been my biggest supporters. I relied on them both for so many things in my life. As I've stated before, we are a very close family. We're always there for one another no matter the situation. Because of that, Molly along with my brother Matt decided to follow me to Lima. They loaded up a truck with most of my belongings.

Guylo and I were in my car leading the way. Once again, Guylo sat in my lap, waiting for a pat on the head or a rub behind the ears. I was constantly reaching out to touch him. Just feeling Guylo's fur seemed to ease my anticipation. With so many thoughts running through my mind, our drive quickly came to an end. We made it to my new home away from home and we tediously unloaded everything from my car and their truck. It was one long and drawn out day. When darkness fell, it was time for Molly and Matt to head home. I hugged them dearly and watched them drive off heading home to Westerville. And just like that, I was on my own.

I was separated from everyone in my life who knew me better than anyone and who I knew and loved more than anyone. That was the very first time I actually needed Guylo. I sat down on the floor. In an instant, Guylo crawled into my lap. I held him for what seemed like hours. Quickly, his fur was covered with tears and kisses. I was so thankful to have my four-legged friend for comfort.

Living independently was an extremely different situation for me. Everyone who I surrounded my life with was now nearly one hundred miles away. Luckily, I had Guylo to get me through the challenges I would face. In the next few months, Guylo and I had grown closer with each passing day. We were practically inseparable.

Many dog owners believe in using crates. They can be wonderful to housebreak puppies or to keep them from chewing items to pieces when you're gone. But I decided against using a crate for Guylo. Instead, he slept right by my side, as if keeping guard. When I left for work, Guylo had the run of our apartment.

I would often come home to find several pairs of shoes all chewed up. I made the mistake of giving him an old shoe to chew on. The problem was, Guylo didn't know the difference between an old shoe and a new one. I quickly learned to shut my closet door. But, it wasn't just shoes. Guylo would find something else to get into. I think he did it on purpose to make me mad, as a way of getting back at me for being gone. It was clear, Guylo did not want me to leave him. He would much rather have me stay with him and not work a day in my life. But, that was obviously impossible. Eventually, he got used to the idea that I had to temporarily leave him. But, I always came home.

I've often heard that dogs do not have a sense of time. For example, you could be gone five hours or five minutes. Within that time, dogs miss you, period. They are just as happy to see you walk through the door after any length of time.

We lived in the upstairs area of a two-story house in Cridersville, a tiny village just south of Lima. It sits in Auglaize County and has a population of nearly two thousand people. Stacey Myers, who was a videographer at WLIO, owned the home. I rented the upstairs apartment from her.

Funny story about Stacey, when I was originally trying to decide where I would live while working at the TV station, I asked her if it would be ok for me to have a dog. She had no problem with it whatsoever. Stacey thought I looked like the type of person who would have a tiny lap dog like a Teacup Maltese or a Yorkie or something like that. Boy, was she wrong. The first time Stacey saw Guylo, she couldn't believe the size of his paws. I think she instantly regretted giving me the green light to keep a dog in her house. However, a part of her had to feel a sense of security. After all, a

11

big, strong, fearless German Shepherd would be living under her roof. That's not a bad thing!

As time went on, it got to the point that I took Guylo almost everywhere. He loved riding in my car. Looking back at it now, I don't think it was the car that he loved. It was probably just the idea of him and I being together. Just us two alone, heading down the open road.

Not only did I choose not to keep Guylo in a crate, I also rarely needed a leash. He always stayed next to me, walking side by side. If he was a few steps in front of me, he constantly turned around just to make sure I was still there. I always was. As our relationship continued to grow, I soon realized that having Guylo in my life was the best decision I ever made. I absolutely loved my pup. He was so well behaved, obedient and so loving. I never needed dog training classes, a leash or a crate. I guess all I really needed was to show Guylo how much I cared.

One day, Guylo and I were on one of our regular walks. We always went on different walking paths or parks because I never wanted him to get bored with the same scenery. The months were colder now and ice was forming on puddles and ponds. Like most dogs, if Guylo saw a squirrel, groundhog or rabbit, he would chase it and then quickly come back to me. But, it would be a goose that nearly ended the wonderful relationship Guylo and I had already formed in such a short amount of time.

We were walking around a nearly frozen pond about a mile from our apartment when all at once, Guylo saw that particular goose land on the pond. No one was near the area. It was just us two. He acted instinctively and ran after it. Problem was, the pond was not completely frozen. The ice around Guylo's paws started to give way and just like that, Guylo was going under the bitterly cold water.

I couldn't believe it. How could this be happening? I couldn't help but come to the realization that this was the end of my new best friend. He was drowning. No one else was in sight. No one was around to help in anyway.

I've heard before how people react in certain situations, not really thinking about the complications or the end result. Well, on that cold winter day, my instincts took over and I trudged into the frigid water to save my dog. Without thinking, I wrapped my arms around his neck and chest and pulled him safely to dry land. We were both out of breath and in shock from what had just happened. I knew that Guylo was most likely freezing and that I should be freezing as well. But, the cold didn't bother me. My body was running on pure adrenilation.

We managed to leave the pond area as soon as we could and went straight home. I hurried out of my wet clothes and changed into a cozy warm robe. I also wrapped my pup into a comfortable blanket. We sat by one another for a long while. From that moment on, I swear Guylo knew exactly what I did. I truly believe he understood that I saved his life.

We were close before the pond incident. But afterwards, an undeniable bond of trust and compassion emerged within Guylo's heart. I became the center of his world. No one or nothing would ever come between Guylo and his savior.

Chapter 4.

GONE

Puppies definitely don't stay little long, especially German Shepherd pups. Guylo was growing by leaps and bounds. He was nearly a year now. Within that time, he grew into one beautiful boy.

One of my favorite things to do was watch Guylo drink water. I know, it sounds pretty boring. But, not the way Guylo drank. I'm not talking about using his dog dish. I'm talking about an actual water fountain. Guylo was so tall, he could stand on his hind legs, put his front paws near the waterspout and drink. Of course, I had to press the button to turn on the water. It was definitely something to see. People around us often pointed and chuckled.

As big as Guylo was getting, he was still so dependent on me. Actually, I depended on him as well, maybe even more. My life would have been so empty if I didn't have Guylo. He truly helped ease the sorrow of missing my family and friends from back home. Because of Guylo, I was never alone.

One of the first friends in the Lima area I met outside of WLIO was named Kim Kelley. Our paths crossed when I was doing a story at a local hospital where Kim worked. I immediately noticed how kindhearted and compassionate she was. Kim quickly introduced me to several other friends. I have always been thankful of how she took me under her wing. What made our friendship even better, she had a dog named Mitz! I've always noticed how moms get together with other moms so their children can play. Well, the same thing happens for dog moms. At least it did with Kim, Mitz, Guylo and me. It was fun for all four of us.

However, as much as we loved hanging out with others, the greatest gift Guylo and I gave one another was our undivided attention. We cherished the precious time we spent together, especially when it was just the two of us.

Guylo loved being outside. I made sure we went on various adventures every day. I didn't want to leave him in my apartment when I went to work. So, I put up a chain link enclosure where he could stay and play while I was gone.

I wanted to test the enclosure before I actually left him in it. I put Guylo in the pen and snuck upstairs to our apartment. I quickly went inside and spied out the window. Within seconds, Guylo had jumped out of the pen and started scratching at the door so he could join me. Not good. I decided to make the chain link walls ten feet tall. There was no way he could jump out now.

My drive to work was about ten minutes. I had different duties at WLIO. For the most part, I was a general assignment news reporter covering everything from fatal fires to city council meetings. I would also get to fill in on the anchor desk for the morning and noon news. My boss would occasionally let me do some sports reporting as well. I have always loved sports so getting to cover various sporting events was right up my alley.

However, more often than not, I did the weather. Yes, it's true. I had no desire to forecast the weather. But, at this particular station and at this particular time, a licensed meteorologist was not needed to do the weather. Basically, anyone could do it. Managers just wanted someone to get the area forecast off the wire service and deliver it to our viewers. They wanted someone who was upbeat and personable and who could also adlib. Apparently, I fit the bill because I was often on the schedule to do the 6pm and 11pm weather. I still covered news stories in between the shows.

However, no matter which shift I worked, I always drove home to Cridersville for my dinner or lunch breaks. I didn't like leaving my boy for that long of a time period. So, most days or nights, I spent my work breaks with Guylo.

For the most part, those breaks were pleasant and uneventful. However, one of those dinner breaks stands out in my mind far more than the others. I pulled up to our apartment after the 6pm news, not expecting anything to be different than all the other times I'd come home. But, this was much different. I couldn't see Guylo in the pen.   Instantly, my heart sank.

He had to be in there. Maybe he was just lying down where I couldn't see him. I got out of my car and ran to the pen. It was empty. The gate was shut and there were no openings where he could sneak out. I was baffled. But, more than anything, I was scared. I looked all around the yard and beyond. Where could he be? There is no way the love of my life would leave me.

Stacey's house was about 150 feet from railroad tracks. I started to panic. Trains were constantly going through Cridersville. My head started to spin. I began asking   neighbors if they had seen Guylo. I stopped

16

everyone who I came across as I headed for the railroad tracks. I couldn't help but fear the worst. I searched up and down the tracks but found nothing. Not a trace of my German Shepherd. I spent the next couple hours going absolutely crazy. Nearly everyone in the small town was now aware that Guylo was missing. But no one knew where he was or didn't remember seeing him walking or running around.

I had to go back to work for the 11pm news that night. My neighbors promised to continue looking. They also promised to call when they found him. I have no idea how I managed to put a forecast together that night, let alone deliver it on live TV. I was half tempted to go on the air and tell all our viewers that my dog was missing. I wanted to show a picture or give a description, but I knew I didn't have the power to do that. Besides, I was sure that one of my neighbors tracked him down and that he was back in his pen. However, no phone call ever came.

As soon as the news ended, I raced home. As I drove, I continued to hope for the best. Maybe, by the time I got home Guylo would be waiting for me. He'd be looking up at me like nothing had happened. No such luck. Guylo was gone.

Once again, I hit the streets looking for him and calling for him. I was so heartbroken and   so confused. How could this happen? In trying times, our minds go everywhere. We often start thinking of various scenarios. I'm not sure why the human race does this, but we often concentrate on the negative, thinking of the worst possible situation rather than the best. I thought someone could have taken Guylo for a dog fighting ring. I was well   aware of horrible people stealing dogs from homes and yards to train their dogs to fight. That idea literally made me sick to my stomach.

Perhaps some punk teenagers took Guylo and were torturing him or maybe they just let him out of his pen as a practical joke and that he ended up getting hit by an oncoming train. If he was still alive somewhere, was he hungry, thirsty, tired or scared? Guylo had an outstanding sense of direction. I knew he would be home if he could be. Someone had to be holding him against his will.

I didn't sleep a wink that night. Finally, morning came. The array of sunlight brought new hope but then reality sunk in. Guylo was still gone. The next day, my Mom and one of my best friends, Brent Axline, drove to Cridersville to console me and to help look for Guylo. I made fliers and put them everywhere. Brent and I walked and drove all over the area while my mom stayed at the apartment in case someone called with information. We didn't have cell phones back then. The only type of communication was my home phone.

No one saw him. No one noticed him. No one heard him. Finally, from the corner of my eye, I saw what looked like a German Shepherd in someone else's yard. The dog was chained up. We moved closer and I knew in my heart that we had just found Guylo. Thank God, my prayers were answered! We were about 25 feet away when he turned to face me. It wasn't Guylo. I was devastated.

My body caved and I fell to the ground. Brent tried to stop my tears, but it wasn't working. How was I going to find my dog? Where in the world could he be? Not knowing was absolute torture. Maybe I just had to face the fact that he was gone and wasn't coming back.

We decided to check in with my mom. Hopefully, someone had called with good news. I needed to get the information in person. So, we headed back to my apartment. As Brent and I started walking up the steps to my apartment, I heard my mom talking to someone. Before I could open the door, Guylo jumped up to greet me! He was back! Guylo was home. I dropped to the ground once again, but this time, in sheer joy. I covered my boy with hugs and kisses and refused to let go.

A young man who worked at a nearby pizza carryout was talking to my mom. Apparently, he delivered a pizza to a house and found Guylo. The people who lived in that home said they saw Guylo walking around the area. He appeared to be looking for something or someone. I knew exactly who he was looking for. Those people took him in and planned to keep Guylo until the Pizza Boy explained the situation. Thank goodness for that young man. He never made a more important delivery. He brought my boy home.

I never found out what happened the day that Guylo went missing. Did he scale a ten-foot-tall chain link wall to get out? Did someone open the gate and let him out? It didn't really matter. I was done with the outside pen. Whenever I left for work, Guylo enjoyed the comfort of our apartment from the inside. At that point, I didn't care how many shoes Guylo wanted to ruin, I was never going through that again. My heart couldn't take it. There was no way Guylo was going to leave me, not if I could help it anyway.

Chapter 5.

MY PROTECTOR

Without question, time only made our relationship stronger. Guylo was more than a year old. Yet, it felt like I had him a lifetime. I often wondered if most people who decided to get a puppy for the first time had this much drama in that first year? It didn't matter. I was committed to Guylo through the good and bad times. Besides, I couldn't imagine my world without my German Shepherd.

When someone saw me, they most likely saw Guylo too. Basically, wherever I went, he went. We were side by side. He always stayed close, almost too close. I remember one time when we were taking a late-night walk after I got home from work. I thought I would test his agility. I would climb on top of structures, playground equipment and other things just to see if he could and would follow. Sure enough, he didn't miss a beat. Guylo would not let me out of his sight. No matter what the obstacle, he'd accept the challenge and stay by my side.

At the end of our walk, on this particular night, I decided to take our nice and easy paced stride up a notch. So, I started to run. I ran as fast as I could for as long as I could. Then, all at once, I stopped. I knew Guylo was close by but I had no idea how close. Within an instant, more than one hundred pounds came barreling into the back of my lower legs. Boom, I came crashing down to the cold, hard unfriendly cement! At first, I didn't know what happened. Where was my dog?

Why did he not protect me against this sharp, shooting pain in my lower body? When I looked up, I had my answer. Guylo was running so close to me that when I came to an abrupt stop, he had no choice but to crash into me. Lesson learned, I never tried that again.

On my days off from work, I often drove home to Westerville. It was so nice to be able to pack up my car and head home. I always looked forward to seeing my family and visiting with my friends. Because I was so excited to go home, getting there seemed to take forever. But, I never once made that drive alone. Guylo always rode in the passenger's seat with his head happily sticking out the window gulping in fresh air along the way.

It was a pretty easy drive. However, one trip home turned out to be a little more adventurous than I ever wanted. That journey home started out just like all the others. The car was loaded up, my radio was on, the windows were down, and Guylo was sitting shotgun. Then, without warning my car came to an abrupt stop. It had broken down.

We sat in silence. No purring engine. No radio. No anything. My car had never given me trouble before. Why now? We were on a back isolated road with only a few houses nearby. As I have mentioned before, I did not have a cell phone. These days, we know how addicting they can be. But, cell phones can also come in handy at times like this. However, I had no choice but to walk to the closest house and ask for help. Luckily, I had Guylo. You never know who will answer the door when you're in the middle of nowhere!

Guylo and I strolled up the long gravel driveway to the lone house which stood about one hundred feet off the street. There was no doorbell, so I knocked. A few moments passed. No one answered. I tried again, still nothing.

Guylo and I turned to walk back to the car and as we were halfway down the driveway, a dark colored car turned into the same driveway heading toward us. When the driver reached us, he rolled down the window. I hesitantly approached the middle-aged man explaining my car troubles. He asked if I wanted to go inside and call a tow company. Was he kidding? I've seen too many movies and read too many news stories to know that there are cold crazy people in this world just waiting for an opportunity like this. An opportunity to attack a stranded young woman and her dog.

I told the man that I couldn't leave Guylo outside alone but asked if he would call. He did. Within twenty minutes, a truck came to drag my car away. Guylo and I rode inside the cab of the truck. We ended up at a car repair shop where I knew no one. The workers fell in love with Guylo as soon as they met him. Within a rather short period of time, my car was fixed and we were once again headed home.

Nothing unusual happened that day. But something inside me often wondered what if. What if I didn't have Guylo in the car with me? You hear so many stories of people being abducted, raped, or beaten in similar situations. I am not a negative person in any way, shape or form. But, working in the news business definitely makes you more aware of your surroundings and you quickly become a realist. I know one thing, I am thankful I was not alone when my car broke down. Guylo had no idea what had just happened. To him, it was just another adventure we faced together and a chance for him to meet new people. But deep down, I knew I could face just about anything with my protector by my side.

Another example of how Guylo came to my rescue took place in the middle of the night at our Cridersville apartment. I was asleep in my bedroom and had no idea what was unfolding on the outside. Apparently, a man, in his twenties, was given a dare and he was about to see it through.

A friend of this man had dared him to climb on top of my roof and spy on me. Word travels extremely fast in a small town like Cridersville. So, when people found out that "the weather lady" was living in the upstairs apartment of the house owned by longtime resident Stacey Myers, regulars were rather intrigued. Somehow, this guy scaled the house and was on the ledge of the structure peering into my window. It just so happened Guylo was staring right back at him. That was enough to startle the man. The next thing you know, Stacey came flying out from where she lived on the main level of the house and exploded on him. Between Stacey and Guylo, that man never came near the property again.

In the beginning, I chose Guylo because I always wanted a German Shepherd. But as time passed, It was becoming more and more evident how truly dedicated and devoted this breed truly is. I realized that I didn't just want Guylo in my life, I needed him.

Things were going really well. I loved my job, I was meeting friends, and I had the best dog in the world. However, I have learned to expect the unexpected. Little did I know, my life was about to change and that perfect partnership between Guylo and me was going to be tested. Eventually though, it would be for the better.

Chapter 6.

INTRODUCING RANDY

As time passes, we get older and we often make choices that will affect the rest of our lives. We each have our own set of morals and standards and things that we choose to believe in.

I grew up a Christian and often attended Sunday service at The Church of The Messiah in Uptown Westerville. I pray on a regular basis and I firmly believe that everything happens for a reason. Every single thing we go through along this path we call life, the good and the bad, is all part of God's plan. I obviously moved to Lima for my job at WLIO. However, in my humble opinion, there was another major reason for that move. And, it was far more important than just a job.

One evening in April, the 6:00 evening news had just ended. Our team just walked off the set after delivering the news, weather and sports. I quickly noticed that a couple of my co-workers were grabbing their softball gloves. I asked Vince Koza, our main sports anchor, what was going on. He told me that he was doing a story on a local basketball star who recently made a professional softball team called The Men of Steel.

The story focused on one man in particular. His name, Randy Kortokrax. Randy was coming to the station so Vince could conduct an interview and get video of him hitting a softball with his very powerful swing. I didn't know Randy at the time, but I knew how much I loved the sport of softball. So, I told Vince that I could help field while Randy hit. Afterall, someone needed to chase the balls.

After retrieving my mitt from my car, another car pulled into the TV station parking lot. An extremely tall man with thick brown hair and a bushy mustache opened the driver's side door and got out. He was hot, I mean really hot! I was 25 years old and never seriously dated anyone. I had crushes and went out on dates but never wanted anything more than that. I had Guylo, who needed a guy! However, there was something different about Randy Kortokrax. I was caught off guard and intrigued to say the least.

After brief introductions, Vince explained to Randy what type of video he needed to go along with the interview. He basically wanted footage of Randy swinging a bat, sending softballs flying into the air. The shoot was going very well. Randy was hitting bombs in the backyard property of WLIO. I was wearing a black form fitting thigh high dress with a long detachable blazer. Isn't funny how we can remember exactly what we were wearing during particular moments? As for shoes, I had to take mine off so I could run down balls that were hit across the field.

I have played softball all my life, from the time I was a little girl through high school. In fact, my junior year at Westerville North High School, we went to the state final four. I was the starting right fielder. We didn't win but it was still one heck of an experience. Regional Champs! I could definitely play ball and managed to catch a few of those bombs, but most flew well past me.

The more I talked with Randy, the more interested I became. Apparently, he felt the same way. Before Randy left, he asked me if I would like to go out sometime. I didn't know it at the time, but that was a rather big move for Randy. As picky as I was, he was even worse.

Randy was a guy's guy. He liked to hang out with his buddies, eat and play softball and basketball, and then eat again! He was definitely not a charmer or what some people would call a "ladies' man". Not because he couldn't be, because that's how he chose to be. Without hesitation, I told Randy that I would love to go out with him sometime.

I didn't hear from Randy right away. Was he playing hard to get or was he just super busy? Either way, I was getting edgy. I finally found someone I could possibly be romantically interested in (for more than one date), but he wasn't picking up the phone and calling me. That actually made me even more interested.

Finally, my phone rang and it was him. He asked if I could go to a Jimmy Buffett concert. I couldn't go. Because I was a newbie at the station, I always had to work weekends and they included extremely long shifts. I would cover news stories all afternoon and then do the weather for the 6pm and 11pm shows.

The idea to go to a concert together didn't work out and neither did the next couple of ideas he had. Finally, we figured out a time where we could get together. A friend of mine named Laura, who I had met in Lima, was going to visit Randy with me. Although, he grew up around the Lima area, Randy was currently living in Cincinnati with a couple of his friends. They had a softball game on a Wednesday night. So, Laura and I drove down to watch him play.

At first, I thought he was pulling a no show! The game was getting ready to start but Randy was nowhere to be found. Seconds before the first pitch, Randy came jogging up to the diamond carrying his cleats. He was late but at least he was there! I pointed him out to Laura who was very impressed. After the game, she was even more impressed. Actually, we both were.

We went to a drive through to grab a quick bite to eat before we went on with the rest of the evening. Randy and his roommates were in their car and Laura and I followed behind. When we went to pay for our food, the lady working the window said that the car in front of us just paid for our meals. Well played Randy, well played. We ended up going out for a few cocktails and dancing and we all had a blast. I really liked everything about him. But, Randy had to pass one major test. The Guylo test.

A couple weeks after Laura and I traveled down to Cincinnati for Randy's softball game, Randy made his way back up to Cridersville to visit me. It was the first time Randy met Guylo. I could tell right away that he was not a "dog person". As handsome, nice, and fun as Randy was, this would never work if he didn't like Guylo. On the flip side, an absolute deal breaker would be if Guylo didn't like Randy. There was no way I would choose a boyfriend over my best friend.

Guylo and I were playing around outside our apartment waiting for Randy to get there. When he arrived, we cautiously walked up to Randy's car. I had already told Randy all about Guylo and couldn't wait for the two to meet. Personally, I have always loved meeting new people. It's kind of who I am. Guylo seemed to share that same trait. He was great with everyone he met and very friendly with adults and kids alike. Randy though didn't know what to think of Guylo, other than the fact that he was a pretty big dog.

I soon found out that Randy never had a dog. He had no idea how absolutely wonderful dogs were and how much joy they can bring to each individual human. Randy learned that life lesson fast. However, as time went on, it seemed Guylo had something to prove. He wanted Randy to know that he came first in my life and Randy second. Randy learned that the hard way.

Chapter 7.

GUYLO VS. RANDY

When I first met Randy that day at WLIO, he was driving through Lima to visit his family who lived in neighboring Putnam County. The bottom line, we lived a good distance apart (a little more than two hours) and weren't able to see one another that often. That was fine with Guylo. My dog seemed to want all my attention one hundred percent of the time and believe me, he got it.

However, I always looked forward to the days when Randy would visit. I enjoyed his company and quickly started to appreciate his sense of humor. Guylo wasn't nearly as enthused with Randy spending time with us. It wasn't that he didn't like or trust Randy. It was just the fact that Guylo didn't want to share me with anyone. In fact, Guylo had a hard time accepting Randy. He often stood or sat between us, never letting Randy get too close.

It got to the point that Randy had to bring Guylo gifts so he would better accept him. He'd bring a big juicy bone and show it to Guylo. Then, and only then, Guylo would temporarily leave my side to feast on the bone. That's when Randy would sneak over to me for a welcoming hug and a kiss. It was actually pretty funny to watch how it all played out. It became part of the routine every time Randy would visit. There were also constant reminders that Guylo had the upper hand.

One incident, in particular, is definitely worth sharing in this book. I had already left for work and Randy was getting ready to head back down to Cincinnati. He grabbed a bite to eat from my little kitchen that overlooked Main Street in Cridersville. Afterward, he took Guylo for a quick walk. All Randy had to do was get Guylo back inside my apartment and he could take off for his drive to Cincinnati. Sounds simple, but it wasn't. Guylo didn't want to go inside and didn't want to obey Randy. This was a familiar scenario between the two. They both seemed to figure out ways to trick and eventually outsmart one another. Personally, those situations became more and more entertaining to watch unfold.

Randy was about to try a scheme that often proved successful. Several times before, Randy would hop in his car and start to drive away. As soon as Guylo saw that Randy was leaving, he'd run over to the car, basically willing Randy to stay. Randy would then get out of the car and both would walk up to my apartment together. Guylo probably thought he won the battle.

It was an odd relationship between the two. Even though they competed for my attention, they also realized that they were stuck with one another and eventually formed a bond of friendship. But, not necessarily on this exact day.

Randy grabbed his keys and walked to his car with Guylo closely watching every move Randy made. The keys were put into the ignition and Randy started the car and actually started to drive away. Guylo didn't waste any time. He ran toward the car, full speed ahead with an idea of his own. Without hesitation, Guylo sank his sharp teeth into one of the tires on

Randy's car. Before Randy even realized what was happening, Guylo ran to the other side of the car and did the exact same thing to another tire! In that split second, Guylo was able to puncture two tires!

Thank goodness Randy is a calm and forgiving person. I'm not sure if any other man would have handled it like Randy did. More than anything, Randy was actually impressed that Guylo's teeth were strong enough to flatten his tires!

I will never forget the phone call I received from Randy a short time later explaining what had just transpired. I couldn't believe it. How the heck could Guylo do that? And, why the heck did Guylo do that? As dog owners, we try to understand our pets as much as possible. For the most part, I think we are pretty good at figuring them out. We know what they want, their likes and dislikes.

In my opinion, Guylo didn't like the idea of Randy interfering with our relationship. However, I think the more Randy was around us, the more Guylo started to enjoy Randy. If I was away at work and Randy left, Guylo would be alone in my apartment until I got home. I really think Guylo wanted Randy to stay that afternoon and he definitely got his way! Guylo won the battle that particular day and Randy got two new tires for his car.

A different type of battle that brewed between my dog and my man was the fight for food. They always say, a way to a man's heart is through his stomach. That was most definitely the case for Randy Kortokrax.

He loves his food! I wasn't much of a cook. I never had to be. My mom always made dinner, so my siblings and I never had the chore of preparing a meal. But, now that I was on my own, I was learning how to cook and actually, becoming pretty good at it. Randy and I didn't go out to dinner very often. We would much rather spend the time eating in my apartment so we could hang out with Guylo.

I never traveled back down to Cincinnati to visit Randy. He always drove the two hours to visit us. It just made more sense that way. As a kind gesture for always making that drive, I liked having a good warm meal waiting for Randy. I enjoyed treating him. Guylo could always tell when Randy was coming to town. I seemed to spend extra time in the kitchen making sure everything was just right. As soon as Randy would walk through the door, he'd grab a plate of whatever I made. More often than not, Guylo would snatch the food off Randy's plate before Randy even took one bite. Randy learned quickly not to turn his back on his plate, or the food would be gone, and gone fast!

One particular afternoon, Randy and I were going to change things up a little bit and decided to grab a quick sandwich and ice cream cone at a quaint little diner in Lima. Guylo rode with us. I didn't want to leave him at home. I knew we would be quick so Guylo could just stay in my car. It was a comfortable day, not too hot or too cold. I figured Guylo would rather sit in my car than sit in the house all alone. We left the windows cracked for him. But, we soon realized that wasn't good enough.

After a few minutes of looking through the menu, we knew which sandwich we wanted. Our waiter approached us. We thought he was getting ready to take our order. He wasn't. He asked if either one of us had a German Shepherd. That was odd. I immediately spoke up and told him proudly that I had a beautiful

Shepherd. The waiter slowly pointed to the front door and asked me if that was my dog. I looked toward the doorway and sure enough, there was Guylo.

He was sitting outside the diner waiting for the door to open so he could come in. Or, perhaps he was just waiting for us to come out. Either way, people on the inside were scared to walk out and people who wanted to walk into the diner refused. I apologized, grabbed my purse and Randy and walked out. We decided to go to a drive through. I had no idea how Guylo squeezed himself out of the window in my car. But, he did. Once again, he got his way!

Chapter 8.

THE CRASH

I once had a book called, "Life's Little Book Of Instructions." It basically gave the reader advice on things people should and shouldn't do if they want to get the most out of life. On one of the pages, it said to own a convertible at one point in your life. Perhaps I had that in the back of my mind when it was time to buy a new car. I bought a beautiful white LeBaron Convertible. The book was right. I absolutely loved it! Guylo seemed to like it too. He no longer stuck his head out of the window. He got to enjoy a full onslaught of air each time we drove with the top down.

One beautiful spring day, I decided to take Guylo to a nearby reservoir so we both could enjoy a long and healthy walk. It was an easy drive along isolated county roads. It should have taken us about 12 minutes to get there, but we never made it to the reservoir.

I was driving our new convertible with the top down singing to the music that was blaring from my car radio. Guylo was sitting anxiously in the back of the car. As we approached several cross streets, I noticed there were no stop signs on my side of the road. And then, all at once it was there. A stop sign that I never even saw until it was too late.

Everything happened so fast and in that moment's notice, I remember telling myself and my trusted furry friend to hold on. We were going to crash. On a road that rarely sees traffic, one lonely car was at the exact same cross street. We were heading west; they were

34

heading south. Instantly, the music in my car came to a silent stop. The only sound coming from that intersection was the pounding crash of our two cars. I would almost compare it to a small explosion. Seconds later, I heard absolutely nothing. I found myself lying in a field and saw several people running toward me. I later found out those people lived close by the intersection and heard the crash. They rushed to the scene to help in any possible way.

Have you ever been involved in a two-car crash? If you have, then you know that it's not something you soon forget. Everything about it, including the sound, sight and smell of it seems to stay with you forever. You just can't shake that sickening feeling.

Those nearby residents who rushed to the scene were asking me all kinds of questions. But, I couldn't answer. I had one thing on my mind, Guylo. I didn't see him anywhere. My head was spinning from the accident, but I had to get up. I once again had to find my boy. When I looked back at my crushed car, my heart sank. Even from a distance, I could tell there was basically no back seat anymore. As much as I couldn't stand the fact of finding Gulyo's body in the wreckage, I had to look. I had to see what I had done. That, in one stupid and careless moment, I had killed my angel.

I started yelling, "my dog, my dog, my dog!" I closed my eyes trying to stop the tears as I staggered to my once beautiful, new car. I somehow willed myself to peer toward the back seat. There was nothing. At first, I was relieved, and then confused. Where was Guylo? An older man cautiously touched my shoulder and asked what type of dog I had. I told him a German Shepherd. He then pointed across the field and street and asked if that was my dog. My mind and body were in shock from the accident itself. But, when I looked in that direction, I saw my boy pacing back and forth and everything was right with the world once again.

Another stranger who rushed to the scene of the crash said he noticed Guylo circling the accident site. In his opinion, Guylo seemed nervous and scared to move close to the scene but he refused to leave the actual site. He refused to leave me. Guylo must have been thrown from the car on impact. My body was sore and my head was pounding. However, nothing was going to stop me from running to Guylo. When I yelled his name, something in him seemed to snap. He moved as fast as he could to reach me. And there we sat. My arms, like so many times before, wrapped around my best friend.

I have a feeling Guylo felt the same way I did when I first saw our wrecked car, thinking he was trapped inside. He didn't know exactly where I was or what happened in that split second of the collision. But, when he heard my voice calling his name, he knew I was ok.

Fortunately, we were not seriously injured. There were no broken bones, only some scratches, bumps and bruises. The people in the other car weren't hurt either. In fact, they felt sorry for me because I had no family living in town and offered to treat me to dinner that night. I didn't accept but the gesture showed such kindness. I was extremely touched by their compassion. Looking back at it now, it all seems so crazy. With the impact of those two cars crashing together, it's hard to believe no one was killed or seriously injured. God definitely works in mysterious ways.

I was so thankful. There is no doubt, my life could have ended that day. I could have easily killed Guylo, or the family in the other car. I'm sure you have gone through a similar situation. Where you can't help but take a step back and realize how wonderful life is. Yes, things go wrong and yes, times can be tough and challenging. However, when we experience a close call like that, we realize how precious life is and how easily it can be taken from us. That's why it's so important to appreciate every single day. Each one that we live through truly is a gift.

At this point in time, I was also growing more and more thankful that Randy was in my life. When I eventually got back to my apartment. I took a long warm shower. I needed to soak my body. I also needed to collect my thoughts before I called home. My mom was going to freak out. It's not easy to tell your parents that you've been in a serious accident in which your car was a complete loss. It would be especially difficult because my mom and dad weren't there to hold me in their arms and comfort my heart.

For some reason, before I called home, I dialed Randy's number. He was genuinely concerned, not just for me, but also for Guylo. He asked if I wanted him to come up to Cridersville to be with us. I said no, that I was fine. Deep down, I really wanted him to be there, but I would never have told him that. It was late. I could have never asked him to spend two hours driving up to see me after he had a rather busy and challenging day of his own. We hung up and he promised to come visit the next day.

I was still shaken and unnerved. That was my first major accident. My new car, that I loved to drive, was crushed. I didn't really know what to do next. I laid down and snuggled with Guylo. There was no doubt, Guylo knew something was different but didn't understand the reality of the crash itself. My boy. My

Guylo. So close to losing him and it would have been ALL MY FAULT. I could not stop thinking about it.

After a few hours, I heard something or someone at my door. It was so late, close to midnight. Stacey had just gotten off work at WLIO. She was coming to check on me. But when I answered the door, it was Randy. He decided on his own to make the late-night drive to be by my side. I was overwhelmed with emotion. I never expected him but was so grateful to have him to hold. For the first time, Randy didn't need a bone to bribe Guylo. We all three sat there in each other's arms for a very long time. I actually think Guylo was glad Randy was there as well.

I'm a big believer of the saying, "what doesn't kill you makes you stronger". Well, Guylo and I both grew a little stronger that day and we also grew a little closer. We had already been through so much together. What other experiences were we going to face with one another? We even seemed to have an ally in Randy. I was sure that whatever life would throw our way, we could handle it. Even the one major change that was about to unfold.

Photos

This is our first picture together!

Mindy and Guylo heading for Lima, Ohio with the
help of siblings Matt and Molly

Saying goodbye to mom and dad before
moving to Lima

Our house (upstairs apartment) in Cridersville (Lima).

A moment of fun in the yard in Cridersville

MIndy and Guylo getting ready to hit the road.

Passenger seat was crushed.

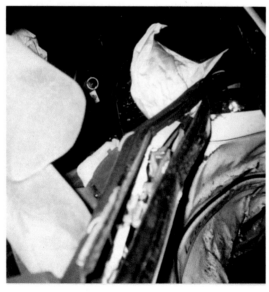

Car crash with Mindy driving and Guylo in back seat.

Taking a water break "Guylo" style!

Guylo relaxing in Westerville

Ta-Dah....Guylo and Mindy
goofing around in their Drayer
family home in Westerville.

Mindy hugs Guylo after coming
home from work at WLIO

Guylo striking a pose. Look at those ears!

Our house in Struthers, Ohio (Youngstown).

Mindy on set at WLIO before a newscast

Mindy and the weekend sports anchor
in the WLIO newsroom

Guylo greeting Randy and looking for a snack!

Guylo in one of Randy's softball jerseys...Defensively,
Guylo could've definitely made the team!

Resting on a bridge after a long walk through
Mill Creek Park

Guylo racing down the cliffs after finding Mindy
in a game of Hide and Seek.

Christmas in Westerville.

Mindy's mom posing with Guylo before a night out

Cheers! On the WYTV news set with
co-anchor Steve Chenevey

Also at WYTV...On the living room style morning show
set with co-anchor Pat Alexander

Trip to Alum Creek Beach when Mindy, Randy and Guylo came back to Westerville for a visit.

Enjoying a moment in Mill Creek Park.

Another shot of Guylo playing softball
(his second favorite love)

If Guylo wasn't chasing softballs, he'd find a stick...
The bigger, the better!

Guylo always had to swim out to Mindy no matter
how far out she would go!

Guylo was always on the alert and ready to protect.
Here, he notices someone coming through the door at
the Westerville house.

Chapter 9.

GOODBYE LIMA

Guylo and I lived in Lima for three and a half years. Within that time, we made wonderful friends and shared countless memories. I learned so much in my first move away from home. However, the time had come to challenge myself professionally. At WLIO, I reported the news on a daily basis, had the opportunity to sit at the anchor desk, forecast the weather and even try my hand at sports reporting. But, I was beginning to feel complacent. I needed something different. I needed to move onto a bigger television market in a different city.

My one main goal was to come home to Central Ohio and work at a Columbus TV station. Just out of curiosity sake, I often sent resume tapes to the three stations in that area, WBNS, WCMH, and WSYX. But I never heard anything. I'm sure I didn't have enough experience for the news directors at those stations to even consider me. So, I had to explore other options.

In my job search, I came across, what seemed to be, the perfect opportunity! An ABC affiliate in Youngstown, Ohio was starting a new morning show and managers were looking for a woman host to co-anchor it.

I didn't know much about Youngstown. Actually, I didn't know anything about Youngstown except for the fact that it's even further away from Westerville than Lima is. Still though, I had to try. I sent a new version of my resume tape. It's so important to keep updating those tapes. News directors want to see your latest work and your best work.

I felt good about the sample I mailed to Youngstown. Most people in the broadcasting business have their own agent. The agents often have close relationships with news directors across the country. They help reporters and anchors find jobs and they can also get both sides to agree on a contract requesting significantly more money and other perks as well. I never had an agent. I always found my jobs on my own which is obviously more difficult. But that feeling of succeeding independently can be a pretty good feeling, very rewarding.

The name of the station in Youngstown was WYTV. In a few days, the news director there was about to see my tape. I couldn't help but wonder if I would get a phone call or not. I was used to never hearing anything after I mailed tapes repeatedly to Columbus. So, I wasn't getting my hopes up. But something inside me felt a little different this time. Youngstown is a much smaller market than Columbus. Perhaps I had enough experience to work there. I would have to wait and see.

For those of you who live in the midwest. Or, for those who have ever spent time there, you know how absolutely beautiful fall is in that region. The leaves turn brilliant colors of orange, yellow, red and even purple. Guylo and I seemed to take longer walks in the fall. We always took time to appreciate our surroundings and appreciate our time together. That beautiful, crisp season was coming to an end and winter was about to set in.

A couple weeks after mailing my tape, Guylo and I were just coming in from one of our walks when I saw the light on my answering machine flashing. I pressed the button expecting to hear my mom's voice. Ever since I moved out, we have always called one another every day or every night. It's good to hear my mom's voice on a daily basis. Whether I'm having a good day or a bad one, mom is there. But, that was not the case this time. Instead, a man's voice was on the machine. He introduced himself as Tom Mock, the news director at WYTV. He complimented my work and asked me to return his call.

I had to time this call perfectly. Since I lived so close to the railroad tracks, passing trains would often make phone conversations difficult because of the thundering noise each one would make while barreling down the track. After collecting my thoughts and waiting for just the right time, I made the call. The number he gave me was his direct line so he answered almost immediately. After a brief conversation, Mr. Mock asked if I could meet him for an interview. On the inside, I was exploding with excitement. However, on the phone, I kept cool and calm. I was possibly getting a chance at change.

Instead of having to drive all the way from Lima to Youngstown by myself, Tom, along with the station's general manager (Ray Maselli), decided to meet me halfway. I couldn't believe the GM was going to be there as well. That was huge! Just so you understand, each television station has several departments and each department has its own manager. For example, the sales department has a sales manager. The news department has a news director and so on. But the general manager is in charge of all the departments. He is basically the president of the entire station. It was a very good sign.

We met at a restaurant off the interstate. When I walked in, they stood up, and motioned for me to sit down. The meeting could not have gone better. They told me that they were starting a new program on weekday mornings and that it would air right before Good Morning America. The name of their program was going to be called "Daystart 33". It made sense, WYTV was on channel number 33.

The show was going to have a magazine style format. The hosts would read the top news stories of the morning from the news set. But there was also another set which was designed to look like a living room. It had a love seat, a chair, a bookshelf and other decorations which made it seem cozy and inviting to the viewer. This was the area where the hosts would interview guests, and banter back and forth about random stories. In fact, a particular segment was going to be dedicated to that, it was called "chit-chat".

Daystart 33 sounded perfect for me. It would give me a chance to sharpen my news anchoring skills so I could continue to deliver the serious stories. But, at the same time, it would allow me to conduct live interviews, while giving me the freedom to showcase my personality and have some fun with our viewers. I thought it was an outstanding opportunity.

It didn't take long for Tom and Ray to make up their minds. They wanted me to be the female host of Daystart 33 and asked if I would accept their offer. I didn't hesitate. I shook both their hands and walked out of that restaurant thrilled and excited. If I had an agent, I most likely could have signed for more money. But for me, it's never been about that. It's more about doing what you love. And, I loved TV news and interviewing people. Letting them tell their story. Afterall, I've always believed that everyone has a story to tell. It just takes the right person to help tell it.

The show was going to debut in January. But, Tom and Ray wanted me to start working in early December. That way, I could be on the air as a reporter a month before the debut of Daystart 33. This would allow the viewers in Northeast Ohio to warm up to me.

This change was definitely a step up in my career and also a step in the right direction toward my final dream destination, Columbus. However, change is never easy and as I turned my car toward Lima, I started to reflect on all the times Guylo and I shared there and all the people we met along the way. Randy stayed with Guylo while I met with Tom and Ray for lunch that afternoon. I couldn't wait to get back to tell them my great news. This next step, though very positive, was going to be very difficult as well.

Chapter 10.

HELLO YOUNGSTOWN

Without question this was an extremely bittersweet time in my life.

Something that has always been a part of who I am, and who I always will be, is my passion for those I care about. I've always been blessed at meeting friends fast and holding onto most of those friendships forever. I absolutely hate saying goodbye. But, the time had come for Guylo and me to pack up and leave Lima.

I genuinely grew to love that charming city in Northwest Ohio and the people who live there. For the first time, I came to depend on others outside of my family and lifetime friends for various times of need. Now, I had to leave those who I became so fond of. It was a tough thing to do. But, at least I was taking a huge part of my life with me, Guylo.

Before making the move to the other northern corner of the state, I took some time to reflect back on some of our memories that came so easily to the forefront of my mind.

I'll never forget playing softball with some of the friends I made in Lima. We played in a league on a designated night of the workweek. I thought it would be a perfect situation for Guylo. He could come to the games and sit on the bench with everyone, kind of like our mascot. I was wrong. Guylo constantly interrupted the games. If I was in the field, Guylo had to be in the field as well. Or, if a ball was hit into the outfield, Guylo would try and chase it down. He would often beat the fielder to the ball. The umpire would stop the game and I would exchange words with my teammate who was supposed to be taking care of Guylo when our team was on defense.

After the first half of the season, Guylo seemed to get used to the situation and did a much better job at simply watching the action from the bench. However, I have to admit, it was quite entertaining watching Guylo try to play softball with the rest of us. I personally think we should have just given him a jersey. He could catch anything!

Another memory that I often look back on is the time I spent with a fun, generous and caring family. Almost as soon as I moved to the Lima area, I grew extremely close with the Bauman's. They lived two blocks north of my apartment in Cridersville. Mr. and Mrs. Bauman were very gracious with their home and their time.

They had two children, Jonathan and Jennifer. Jonathan was away at school most of the time that I lived in Cridersville. Jennifer was younger and I treated her like she was my little sister. To top it off, the Bauman's had a dog named Spanky. Spanky was a thin and wiry German Shepherd/Husky mix with one blue eye. She was a friendly, fun, frisky dog that happened to be head over heels in love with Guylo.

Jennifer and I would get our dogs together as much as possible. The Bauman's had a swimming pool. So, during the hot and sticky summer days, we would hang out at their house. Both dogs weren't quite sure whether they should join us in the water or not. They mostly just sat at the edge of the pool watching us soak up the sun.

During the other times of the year, the four of us (Jennifer, Spanky, Guylo and I) would all hang together at my place, go on walks or play tennis. No matter where we went, Guylo and Spanky were with us. Since Spanky was part Husky, she loved to run. In fact, when given the chance, she'd often slip away from her home to roam the streets of Cridersville. Whenever she would come up missing, the Bauman's knew where she would end up...my house!

We never had to worry about those two having puppies. Guylo was neutered and Spanky was spayed. Trust me, I know how many unwanted dogs and puppies are living on the streets in every city of our country. It breaks my heart to think of the thousands that are put down every year because they couldn't find homes. The last thing I want to do is add to those stats.

Every dog I've had and will continue to have will always be spayed or neutered. It's just not worth the risk. In any case, saying goodbye to the Baumans and Spanky was very difficult. It was extremely comforting having a family live so close to Guylo and me especially when my family seemed so far away.

Of course, saying goodbye to the dear people who I met at WLIO was extremely painful as well. A lot had happened in the last three and a half years. This small group of friends became such a major part of my life and I was thankful for all of them in their own specific way.

Do you remember at the end of the movie The Wizard of Oz when Dorothy turns to the Scarecrow and says she would miss him most of all? That's how I felt about my closest friend Joe Miles. Joe had the kindest heart and the best sense of humor. We became friends on the very first day I started working at the television station. Our friendship grew stronger each year.

Joe was thirteen years older than me and was a videographer at WLIO. We were often paired up to cover stories together. While on the job, I think we laughed a lot more than we worked. I don't think Joe ever owned a dog when he was growing up. So, he was never crazy about them. However, it didn't take long for Joe to change his tune, at least when it came to my dog. He really didn't have a choice. We spent a great deal of time together on and off the job. He jokingly referred to Guylo as "Dingo Dog".

One beautiful afternoon, Joe, Guylo and I were at the park playing tennis. Joe's sister wanted to come to the park to visit us. So, she did. The problem was, Joe's sister was scared to death of dogs. As she came into the fenced in area where the tennis courts were, Guylo started trotting in her direction as a friendly greeting. Joe's sister freaked out! I've never seen someone run so fast! She scaled that fence in two seconds and kept running far away from the tennis courts. Joe and I laughed so hard. It was one hilarious image I will never erase from my mind.

Although Joe grew up never really being fond of dogs, he changed because of Guylo. He learned to like, trust and even admire Guylo. Dogs, in general, can do that. They can fill a void that no other animal can. All you need to do is open your heart and give a dog a chance. I'm so glad Joe did. But now, Guylo and I were leaving our dear friend behind.

My final week in Lima was a whirlwind. I took mental pictures of all the places that became so familiar to me. The places that I often took for granted, were about to be nothing more than a distant memory. Every police officer, sheriff's deputy, public official or politician who I crossed paths with that week wished me well. I liked everyone so much. I couldn't help but get a little choked up after each of my goodbye hugs. I knew that there was a good chance I may never see these people again. For someone who is extremely people oriented, that's a hard situation to deal with.

The most touching gesture caught me off guard. I wasn't expecting this at all. I was assigned to cover my final Lima City Council meeting. I had covered these meetings on a regular basis and became quite close with many of the members. I walked into the council chambers, but it was empty. Not one member was sitting in their assigned seat. Instead, they were holding an executive session in a small room right next to the main chamber area.

Members of the media were not permitted in those executive sessions. Joe was my photographer that night. He was acting a little odd but I couldn't quite put my finger on it. I just thought he was sad because this was one of our last stories we were going to cover.

Finally, council members came out of the closed-door meeting and, one by one, found their regular seats. The meeting started the same way they had so many times before. I knew the procedure by heart by now. But then, Council President Keith Cunningham stepped up to the microphone and addressed the entire crowd of Lima residents and concerned citizens.

The words started to fall in place and Joe quickly turned his camera away from the council itself and focused on me. What in the heck was Keith saying? And then, it hit me. I couldn't believe and never in a million years would have guessed that Lima City Council would do such a meaningful thing for me.

Council thoughtfully passed a resolution in my honor. How crazy is that? I'm actually in the record books in Lima, Ohio. I tried so hard to hold in my emotions but no such luck. I lost it. I was touched beyond belief. When Keith was done reading it word for word, he made his way to wear I was weeping with pride. I hugged him tightly and then continued to hug each one of those members. They gave me a framed copy of that resolution. I still have it today. This is how it reads:

RESOLUTION - Expressing the appreciation of The Lima City Council to Mindy Drayer upon her resignation from WLIO Television. WHEREAS, Mindy Drayer, a native of Westerville, Ohio, joined the staff of WLIO television August 18, 1992: and Whereas, Mindy Drayer has effectively presented the happenings of the community in her capacity as weather reporter, morning anchor, and news reporter including excellent coverage of Lima City Council action; and WHEREAS, Mindy has resigned her position with WLIO and has accepted a position as co-host of a morning show with WYTV, an ABC affiliate, out of Youngstown, Ohio; now therefore. BE IT RESOLVED BY THE COUNCIL OF THE CITY OF LIMA:

Section 1. That the Council of the city of Lima does hereby extend its appreciation to Mindy Drayer for the capable way in which she has performed her duties in reporting news of local government to the Limaland area, and extend best wishes to her in her future endeavors.

Section 2. That the Clerk is authorized and directed, upon adoption of this resolution, to provide a copy to Mindy Drayer, the Allen County Historical Society, and the local news media.

Section 3. That the Clerk of Council is authorized to cause publication of this resolution is a summary manner as provided by the City Charter.

Section 4. That this resolution shall take effect and be in force from and after the earliest period allowed by law.

I'm sure you understand why I was so touched. When people move away from home for a job, I don't think they really expect to become attached to so many people. Often times, men and women will accept a job as a steppingstone. They plan to live in a new unfamiliar city while punching the clock at their new workplace. But, in many cases, friendships are created, and memories are made and just like that, bonds are formed. That is exactly what happened to me.

The end was here. My time in Lima was over. It just so happened that the company Christmas party was my final swan song. The gathering provided the perfect setting for one last goodbye to everyone I worked with. We all were dressed up for the festive occasion. We ate, drank and even danced a little as well. Some, more than others. I was always ready in any situation to steam up a dancefloor! In fact, I've always felt that in life, there are dancers and those who watch others dance. Don't be a gawker, be a dancer. Like the Lee Ann Womack song says, "I Hope You Dance."

My boss, the man who took a chance on me several years before, stood in front of our entire staff and recited a small speech about how I was heading to Youngstown and how the station, the city and the people will miss me as a reporter but more as a person. It was the perfect ending to a time in my life that I recall so vividly. A time that I am so grateful to have had. I was sad to leave but ready for my next challenge.

That next step started with a challenge of its own. It was absolutely the coldest night of the winter season when we drove from one end of Ohio to the other. Randy, Guylo and I managed to load up three and a half years of memories into our cars. Two dear friends from Lima, Christina and Jason, graciously volunteered to travel with us in another car carrying more of my belongings.

Finally, we arrived at my new home away from home away from home. It was a small ranch style light brick house that I would be renting from an elderly couple who lived about a half mile down the road. With an arm load of boxes, I unlocked the door. We couldn't wait to get out of the bitterly cold whipping wind.

But, as soon as we stepped inside the house, we knew something was surprisingly wrong. The house wasn't much warmer than the outside.

We soon came to realize the structure had no heat and there was no fixing the problem until the next day.

Basically, the first memory I have of my move to Youngstown was trying desperately to stay warm while I slept in my new surroundings. I could literally see my breath each time I opened my mouth! I remember piling as many blankets, towels and robes on top of me and often using a hair dryer under the covers trying to generate my own heat. But one thing seemed to work better than anything. Guylo laid beside me all night long. He kept me warm. Once again, I realized how much I needed my big, strong, loving dog. He was my angel.

Morning came and finally, the heating problem was fixed. Christina and Jason were well on their way back to Lima. Randy stayed with Guylo and me to explore Youngstown and the beautiful surroundings of Mahoning County.

We bundled up and hit the outdoors. I needed to find parks, paths and fields where Guylo could run free. It didn't take long. This city that was once known for its booming steel mills and factories, had another side to it. Absolutely beautiful valleys, trees, hillsides, and streams are nestled in this northeast corner of Ohio. It's called Mill Creek Park and it's one of the best attractions in Youngstown. The park is made up of 4,400 acres and is one of the largest inner-city parks in America. Plus, it's absolutely gorgeous. The winding walking paths are breathtaking. I had a feeling Guylo and I were going to get to know every inch of it.

Chapter 11.

Y-TOWN IS MY TOWN

In life, we don't always get to choose the path we walk down. Many times, those paths choose us. Out of all the cities in the world I could have chosen to live, Lima and Youngstown may not have been at the top of my list. But, those were the places that offered me opportunities to further my career. And, in both cases, I learned to love those cities and the people in them. We have to make the most out of those opportunities. Hopefully, in the end, it will all make sense and those little steps along the way will lead to something bigger and better. But, until that happens, it's so important to enjoy each moment and each part of that journey.

I was starting to gain more and more experience reporting the news. The name of the show I was hired to co-anchor was called Daystart 33. It was a local news program that aired weekday mornings on the ABC affiliate in Youngstown, WYTV. Sleeping in quickly became a thing of the past. Not only did I have to get used to crazy early morning hours, so did Guylo.

The best part of the shift was having the majority of the days and evenings off. That way, I could dedicate even more time to my best friend. Aside from work, Guylo and I were together all the time.

One of the most exciting challenges when moving to a new location is meeting people. I was quickly introduced to all my co-workers at the station. They were good, hard working people who took pride in their jobs. However, other friendships grew between the people I met outside of work as well.

It's funny how sometimes you meet people, and something automatically clicks. There's an instant feeling of companionship, trust and often times admiration. That's exactly how I felt the moment I met Phil and Marilyn Chuey They were old enough to be my parents and they seemed to look after me and made me feel so welcome and accepted in my new city.

Phil and Marilyn were huge dog lovers and had a beautiful golden retriever. In fact, all of us spent a lot of time together. We would meet at one of the many Mill Creek Park locations and simply walk and talk. The dogs seemed to cherish their time together just as much as we did.

The Chuey's were extremely active for their age and were truly dedicated to one another and to the dogs they owned over the years.

They were good people to know. Afterall, Marilyn's father was the very first president of Youngstown State University. I remember thinking to myself that if Randy and I were to ever get married, I wanted our marriage to be like theirs.

Being physically fit has always been important to me. That's one reason why Guylo and I walked so much. But, I was about to be given another opportunity to stay in shape and it was all because of Guylo.

I was doing a story on New Year's Eve resolutions and people who promised to keep them this time around. I needed to find a fitness expert who could offer tips on how to make exercise resolutions last throughout the entire year rather than only the first three months.

After a few phone calls and suggestions, I met with a woman body builder who owned her own gym. It was in a medium sized space on the second floor of an office building. Her name was Jeanette Estremera. We hit it off right away. She was fun, energetic and had a great personality. Plus, she was an expert on fitness advice. You could tell that right away.

I was so impressed with Jeanette and her gym, I started working out there. Soon after our initial meeting, I introduced her to Guylo. Jeanette was a big dog lover as well. So much so, she gave me a key to her gym and told me to work out whenever I wanted, even after hours. This way, I could bring Guylo with me. It was a wonderful arrangement.

Whenever I hopped on the treadmill or bike, Guylo stayed right beside me. When I moved to the free weights, he moved with me as if guarding my every move. I never had to fear walking into the poorly lit office building and then climbing the isolated staircase. I had my trusted guard dog. It was very generous of Jeanette to make that accommodation for me. Guylo seemed to bring out the best in people. Anyone who met my dog, seemed to become a better person because of it.

However, there was one situation that happened inside Jeanette's gym that I will never forget. Not many people know about the incident until now.

It was a relatively normal evening. I was working out with Gulyo by my side when Randy called. He was on his way to Youngstown for a surprise visit. Shoot! I had no groceries at the house and Randy is a huge eater.

Fortunately, there was a 24 hour market right beside the gym. Instead of putting Guylo in my car while I got some groceries, I left him at Jeanette's place. It was more spacious than my car and he was comfortable there.

It didn't take too long to buy what I needed from the store. I headed back to the gym to finish my workout and grab Guylo. But, everything changed the moment I walked through the door.

The sight and smell hit me like a ton of bricks! Guylo had a terrible case of diarrhea. I mean, it was everywhere! I quickly called Randy. He was in the area by now and he immediately came to help. Together, we scrubbed and scrubbed and scrubbed. At the time, we were in panic mode. What if Jeanette decided to come to her gym? What if we couldn't get the mess cleaned up? What if Guylo had to go to the bathroom again?

It took a couple hours but eventually, we managed to get the job done. Eventually, the floor was cleaned and the room was saturated with air freshener. We went home. Jeanette never seemed to notice. If she did, she never questioned me. But it was a major bonding moment between Randy, Guylo and me. We were so thankful that it was over. However, Guylo didn't quite seem like himself. I had no idea that it was the beginning of the end.

Chapter 12.

DISTANCE MAKES
THE HEART GROW FONDER

Guylo and I were becoming more and more comfortable in Youngstown. We were meeting new friends every day and exploring countless corners of Mill Creek Park. Randy was traveling a lot from Cincinnati to Youngstown. It was a long and tedious drive. But, he was willing to make that sacrifice as often as possible to spend quality time with us.

One of our favorite things to do was play hide and seek. Randy would hold on to Guylo while I hid. As soon as Guylo was free, he ran as fast as he could to find me. He always won that game.

Yes, Randy was extremely dedicated to Guylo and me. But, he was passionate about playing ball as well. He should be, it was his job. Randy was fortunate enough to travel the country playing softball. Believe it or not, that's how these big, beefy guys made a living. They were paid good money to play SLOW PITCH softball. At the time, it was a big business and Randy could hit a ball further than just about anyone in the country.

As many of you know, the more you do something, chances are, the better you become. When Randy made his trek to Youngstown, you can bet the three of us found an empty softball field and used it as often as possible. Randy wanted to work on his swing. After all, his main job on the team was to hit it out of the park.

You may be wondering how batting practice was possible with a guy, a girl and a dog. Well, we made it work. And, it worked well. As I earlier stated, I have always loved the game of softball. It was rather fitting that we three spent so much time together on a softball field.

In this current situation, I would pitch. Randy would hit, and Guylo would field. I'm not kidding. We did this almost every time Randy came to town. It was a blast, until the one time when Randy hit one up the middle nearly taking my head off! But, that's a different story for another book!

Looking back at it now, I can only imagine what the three of us looked like out on those softball fields. Guylo never quit. He ran and ran and ran after those balls. He would chase them down grab them with his mouth and bring each ball back to me on the pitcher's mound. By the end of each round, Guylo was, by far, the most worn out.

Remember when I first got Guylo when he was a puppy? The breeder told me his pups needed a job. I think this was Guylo's job and he was never going to let Randy and I down. That's just the way Guylo was. At the end of this book, you'll find out what I believe Guylo's most important job was. But that isn't until the final chapter.

Looking at Randy's softball schedule, we noticed his team was playing in a tournament in Cleveland. That's not too far from Youngstown and I really wanted to see Randy play. A couple of my friends wanted to go as well. My friends and I thought it would be fun for all of us to get a hotel room for the weekend. The problem was, I didn't want to leave Guylo. I had never left him overnight before. I was really torn, until a woman from work came up with an idea.

Her name was Brenda and she was a huge animal lover. She lived on a farm and had chickens, ducks, horses, cats and dogs. She said Guylo could stay with her while I went to Cleveland. Guylo and I drove to her property so we could check it out. I wanted to make sure it was a good fit for my best friend. It was a wonderful location out in the country. It was absolutely perfect for pets. It had several acres of land with a small pond. I knew Guylo would be happy. He could run all day and play with the other animals. After a little coaxing, I agreed.

A couple days later, Guylo and I returned to Brenda's farmhouse. But this time, I left him there. It was such a hard thing to do. I had to get in my car and drive away with Guylo watching the car disappear down the long winding gravel road. I knew eventually, he would be fine. He'd end up playing with the other animals and I trusted Brenda. She was a great person with a compassionate heart.

I tried not to think about it while I was in Cleveland with my friends. I enjoyed watching Randy dominate on the field. Overall, everyone had fun. It was nice to get away for a couple days. But, deep down, my heart ached for my angel. I couldn't wait to pick up Guylo so both of us could head home and be together again.

The drive to Brenda's seemed to take forever. Finally, I pulled up to the house. I thought I would see Guylo running around or playing on the property. But, I saw nothing. Finally, I noticed some of the other pets out and about, but still no Guylo.

I quickly parked my car and walked up to the front door. Without hesitation, Brenda answered. "Thank goodness you're here" were the first words out of her mouth. I asked where Guylo was and she simply pointed to the corner of the kitchen.

He seemed so sad and despondent. He had no idea I was there. I started to move toward him while saying his name. All at once, he tilted his head and jumped to his feet. Within a moment's notice my big, beautiful boy was back in my arms.

Brenda was in disbelief. She explained to me how difficult the weekend was on Guylo. She begged and pleaded with him to play with the other animals, walk with her or eat something. But he refused to cooperate. Guylo didn't eat one bite or move a muscle the entire time I was gone. Brenda said Guylo laid in the same spot from Friday through Sunday.

I'll never forget the words Brenda told me as Guylo and I were getting into my car. She turned to me and said, "Mindy, I have been around animals all my life and I have never seen a bond like that. I've never seen a dog so attached to someone." Her words made me feel good yet guilty at the same time. I knew in my heart that Guylo and I had a relationship few would understand. And, I also knew how difficult it was going to be when one day we would have to part forever.

Chapter 13.

SO LONG YOUNGSTOWN

My time in Youngstown went faster than expected. Personally, the city treated me well. I made wonderful friends who I loved spending time with. Randy eventually moved to Youngstown as well and rented a place of his own. He had a degree in education and accepted a teaching job in the city school system. Of course, that meant Randy and I saw one another on a regular basis. In fact, I had come to the conclusion that this would most likely be the man I would one day marry.

Professionally, things weren't bad, but they weren't great. I enjoyed anchoring the weekday morning news. However, something was missing. I still wanted so badly to move home. I never gave up trying to land a job at one of the television stations in Columbus. I continuously sent updated resume tapes. Unfortunately, things weren't working out in my favor.

Careers in TV news are constantly changing. Anchors and reporters are always looking for better opportunities in bigger cities. Managers come and go quite often as well, especially news directors and general managers.

WYTV was about to go through a major change. A new general manager was taking over. That meant drastic changes could unfold. A GM is a lot like a head coach. They like to put the best possible team together to win. The difference is, they're not trying to win a game. They're hoping to win viewers and eventually ratings.

It wasn't very long before the changes most of us were afraid of took place. Nearly everything I really liked about the morning show was dismantled. The fun, lighthearted interviews to the entertainment and pet segments were all scrapped. This new boss wanted a morning show with no personality. She wanted a straight-forward newscast with traffic and weather every five minutes. Eventually, she wanted new anchors as well.

I was crushed. Her plan was to move me out of the weekday morning anchor chair and put me on the weekend evenings doing weather reports. What?? I am not a meteorologist and have never studied the science of weather forecasting!!! I did weather reports in Lima. But, that was different. All the reporters there tried their hand at forecasting.

I left work that day with a sickening feeling in my gut. The only reason I moved to Youngstown was for the fun morning show job. Now, it was gone. As soon as I walked into my home, Guylo was there to greet me. Some things never change. I curled up on the couch with my big buddy right by my side. Of course, Guylo had no idea what had just transpired at work. Still though, he knew something was different. He could sense my disappointment. I truly believe that dogs have a sixth sense. They seem to empathize with their loved ones more often than not. They understand the human heart more than most people do.

I've needed Guylo so many times in the past. I needed him now again, probably even more than before. He was a constant companion of trust and compassion. In a world where people often prove that they're not what they seem, dogs are the complete opposite. People can walk on you, chew you up and spit you out while a dog will lift you up and heal your wounds.

A lonely feeling of failure kept creeping up on me. I had to do something. But what? I needed to work but I didn't want to do weekend weather. If only I could find another job. That was the answer.

I decided to take two weeks off from work. It was definitely a risk. Those two weeks totaled all my vacation time for the year. I told my news director that I needed time to consider the proposed change to my schedule and position. But, I was actually planning my attack.

Over the next two weeks, I planned to drive to other TV stations across Ohio and personally deliver my resume tapes. I would take a chance. Sometimes, chances are worth taking. In my humble opinion, that's a big part of life. I feel sorry for those who stay in their own safe worlds and never take chances. As the saying goes, "You never know until you try."

I drove to three different cities in Ohio. They were Dayton, Toledo and Columbus. I had a friend who worked at a TV station in Dayton. He was able to get me in the door. However, there were no immediate openings in Dayton.

But, there was an opening in Toledo. I drove to the northwest corner of the state with high hopes. Fortunately, the news director had some free time and decided to meet with me. I really liked him and he seemed to like my work. He gave me a tour of the station. I got to see the studio, newsroom, production booth and edit bays. He also took the time to introduce me to his reporters, photographers and anchors who were working that day. I had a rather strong feeling about a possible job opportunity there.

Next, I drove home to Columbus. I knew it was a long shot. I had tried so many times to land a job in the city where I grew up. Why would this be any different?

They say, to never burn any bridges. That is how I have constantly lived my life. Little did I know, one of my dear friends who I worked with in Lima was about to do something extremely kind. That something would change everything.

Laurie Omness worked at WLIO for years. She knew all the major players in various TV markets across Ohio. She talked to assignment editors throughout the state on a regular basis. They each would share stories and news tips with one another.

One day, Laurie was on the phone with a man named Stan Sanders. At the time, Stan was a main newsroom manager at WCMH, the NBC affiliate in Columbus. Laurie knew that I was looking for a new job and she told him about me. Laurie believed in my work and she made Stan interested in possibly bringing me on board. In fact, she told him that WCMH should hire me before another Columbus station does. Because, in her words, I was going to make it back to Central Ohio one way or another.

Just like that, a meeting was set up between Stan and myself. I eagerly drove down to the square shaped building on Olentangy River Road. I was armed with nothing but my personality and resume tape.

The first person I met was very welcoming. His name was Phil Schneid. He was another manager who came out to the lobby to greet me. Phil walked me through the station and back to the newsroom. It was such an exciting experience. I absolutely loved being inside the walls of this building. I knew this was where I was meant to be.

Phil quickly introduced me to Stan, and both let me join the rest of the staff for their morning meeting. These meetings can be informative and intense. Managers, producers, reporters and anchors all come together to discuss what everyone will do that day including the various stories that need to be covered.

After more brief introductions, Stan and I watched my resume tape together. He didn't say much at the time. He was a hard man to figure out. He told me that the News Director, Jim Sanders was not there that day. I was disappointed. However, that feeling of rejection shifted when Stan explained how the station was looking to grow its reporting staff. NBC4 had a couple openings. Not just one, but a couple! I was so excited. I left that building that day with a wonderful feeling. Nothing was offered to me. I didn't even meet the news director, but something in my gut gave me a feeling of hope and encouragement.

A few days later, my phone rang. It was the News Director at NBC4. He introduced himself to me and apologized for not being at work when I stopped by the other day. He asked if I could be in his office the following day. I hung up the phone, grabbed my parents and thanked God. News directors don't call you unless they're really interested. My hunch was right. I started working at NBC4 in February of 1998.

What does all this have to do with Guylo? Everything! If you allow them to, dogs go through everything with us. They aren't just a bystander watching life happen. They're included along your personal path with every step you take.

As you've read throughout these pages, that's how Guylo and I were. I cannot tell you how many times I'd take him on walks talking about my situation. I explained to my trusted friend how I wanted us to move home to Central Ohio.

Guylo made every two-hour car ride with me, first from Westerville to Lima and then from Westerville to Youngstown. Finally, those car rides were coming to an end. We were going home together. We'd have new parks, places and paths to discover. We'd also rediscover the places where I grew up and were more than familiar with. They'd take on a whole new meaning now though.

I talked to Guylo about everything I experienced over the last several years. Now, I would be telling my loving and loyal German Shepherd all about my good days and bad days at NBC4. We'd also talk about the joys we would share in our everyday lives. Our new adventure together was about to begin. Guylo was my one constant companion in those years of change since college graduation. One final blow was about to occur. This one came out of nowhere and broke my heart indefinitely.

Chapter 14.

GONE, BUT NEVER EVER FORGOTTEN

How come you can't have it all in life? When things seem to be moving along perfectly, just the way you want, something happens to disrupt everything. A good friend once told me, "God laughs when you make plans." That friend was former Ohio State Football Coach Jim Tressel. He's now the president of Youngstown State University. Well, he was right. I had planned on moving home with Guylo. We'd stay side by side through all our new adventures. He had met so many of my friends and co-workers in Lima and Youngstown. Now, he'd get to see more of my childhood friends and be introduced to new co-workers. That's how it was supposed to be. Guylo was only six years old. We still had a lot of time together. Once again, I'm reminded of that prophetic quote, "God laughs when you make plans."

It was a very rewarding and exciting time in my life. After trying for several years to get a job at a Columbus television station, it was finally happening. As I've done before, I packed up everything for yet another move. Hopefully though, this was the final move I would make. My goal was to work back home in Columbus. That's all I really ever wanted. That's what I had worked so hard for.

Finally, the time had come for Guylo and I to hop into my car and head back to Central Ohio. Randy drove behind us in his own car. Both vehicles were once again filled with moving boxes and plenty of memories.

Before leaving Youngstown, we drove around the city taking one last look at the beautiful parks that we walked through so many times before. Those were the areas that we spent so much of our time making countless, wonderful memories each season. We also said our final goodbyes to the people who became so important in our lives. Eventually, we turned our cars toward home. We were on our way!

Throughout my entire life, my parents have always been so considerate, giving and generous about absolutely everything. At this pivotal point in my life, they again came through for me.

My mom and dad were letting Guylo and I move back with them for as long as we needed or wanted. My mom seemed to accept the idea of having us back home a lot easier than my dad. In fact, she was thrilled. But, eventually Dad too realized it was the right thing to do. Funny how sometimes things really do come full circle. After several years of living on my own in Lima and Youngstown, here I was going back to the exact same house where I grew up. Only this time, I'd have a big German Shepherd with me.

With any new job, the first several days are hectic. It takes awhile to learn the ins and outs of how things are done on a daily basis. I wasn't sure exactly what my hours would be at NBC4 or how long I would have to stay at the station each day.

Because of the unknown, I asked Randy to take care of Guylo during that brief time period. Randy was still working in Youngstown and by now, those two had formed a pretty close bond of their own.

Randy is one of the most laid-back, easy going people I've ever known. He was more than happy to take Guylo back to Youngstown while I got used to things at NBC4. It was only going to be for the first few days. Randy would then drive Guylo back down to Columbus over the weekend. It seemed like a perfect plan. Remember, "God laughs when you make plans."

There are various traditions that families all across the world share. One of my favorite Drayer Family traditions is Sunday night dinner. Each Sunday, our entire family gets together to eat, talk, laugh and argue. That's what families do right? At least, that's what my family does. Even when I was living away, I tried coming home for as many of these dinners as possible.

But this time, it was going to mean so much more. I wouldn't have to rush back to Lima or Youngstown at the end of the meal. I was home, back at the same Debbie Drive house my family had lived in since 1972. However, Randy and Guylo did have to head back. I hated to see them go.

For some reason, I had a very strange feeling in my heart and in my head that evening. I kept thinking it was just a sense of nerves and anxiety. I was about to start my new job and be on the air in Central Ohio where so many of my friends, family, teachers, and neighbors could see me.

Or, maybe that uneasy feeling was something entirely different. I've always heard to trust your gut. My insides were definitely trying to tell me something. I just didn't know what that something was.

As my family finished eating and cleaning up the kitchen, Randy and Guylo were getting ready to drive back to Youngstown. That uneasy feeling that I just couldn't shake seemed to take hold within Guylo as well. He stayed unusually close to me.

Guylo was very comfortable at my parents' home and had the freedom to wander about, which he normally did. But not on this particular evening. To be honest, Guylo always stayed close to me, but this was different. My dog had become my constant shadow, following my every single move. I have always believed that dogs have a sense of wisdom far beyond what humans can understand. Guylo knew something, there is no doubt about it.

Although we kept putting off that final moment, it was time for Randy and Guylo to climb into the car and head to the northeast part of the state.

Our embrace seemed to last forever. Looking back at it now, I wish that it did. When we all let go, Randy got into the driver's seat and my faithful German Shepherd made his way to the back of the car. That unsettling feeling of uncertainty was even stronger now. I couldn't help myself. I motioned for Guylo to jump back out of the car so I could hug and kiss him once again. He didn't hesitate. I stroked his fur and held his head in my arms just like I had done so many times before. But, I swear, this time was different. It was like I was assuring him that everything would be fine. I also told him that we'd be back together in a few days.

Guylo seemed to understand, at least I thought so. He got inside the car again and I slowly closed the door. And, just like that, Randy and my big, beautiful boy started driving down the street. Guylo refused to look away from me. He stared out the back glass window until the car turned onto a cross street taking them out of my neighborhood. I stood motionless. Even now after all these years, I still see Guylo's face staring back at me while driving down that road. I will never forget that moment. It is etched in my mind and in my heart forever.

The moment Randy and Guylo returned to Youngstown, Randy called to say they made it back safely. I was relieved yet still unsettled. I went to bed that night with so many mixed emotions. I could hardly sleep. My mind was working non stop, thinking of so many different things. I was about to start my new job in a matter of hours. The job I had wanted for so long, back in my hometown in Central Ohio. However, I was trying to sleep without my constant companion lying near me. Normally, anytime I faced change in my life or a challenging situation, Guylo was with me. He was always right by my side when I needed him,

When my eyes finally closed, they were forced back open almost immediately. Off in the distance, I heard my parents' home phone ringing. Remember, I didn't have a cell phone back then. I looked over at the alarm clock. It was a little past 1:00 in the morning. Who would be calling at that time? I jumped out of bed and rushed downstairs. When I answered the phone, I was stunned to hear Randy on the other line. "I don't want you to panic. I don't want you to worry, but Guylo and I are at the veterinarian's office"

"What? Why? What happened?" is all I could say. Randy explained that Guylo ate some dog food when they got out of the car after their drive back to Youngstown. Afterward, Randy thought Guylo didn't seem right. He kept walking in circles and appeared very uncomfortable. Randy wasn't going to take any chances. He found an after-hours pet emergency center. He put Guylo in the car and drove there as fast as he could.

Once at the office, a very compassionate veterinarian approached Randy and Guylo. She did several tests and came to the conclusion that Guylo's stomach had flipped. He needed emergency surgery. Randy called me and handed the phone to the doctor. She explained the situation and told me that she could not operate without getting my consent. There was really no option. I told her to operate and to call me as soon as the surgery was over.

I hung up the phone. I prayed and I cried. I cried and I prayed. All I kept thinking was that I wasn't there. I wasn't with Guylo when he needed me most. All those times when I desperately needed someone or something, Guylo was the one I leaned on. The one constant part of my life that I could count on.

Now, the tables had turned, and I let my best friend down. I promised to make it up to him as soon as possible. I knew he would forgive me. Dogs always do. They are the most trusting, caring, compassionate creatures that God has created. After all, God is dog spelled backwards. They live their lives loving, protecting, pleasing and forgiving. I've always said that if people were more like dogs, this entire world would be so much better.

The next step for me was extremely difficult, the waiting. It was a helpless empty feeling. I could do absolutely nothing but sit by and let time pass. Of course, there was no way I could fall back asleep. So, I just sat alone with my mind racing.

I thought back to the very first time I saw Guylo. I visualized that adorable puppy face, knowing he was perfect for me. I kept thinking of how easily we connected and formed an unbelievable bond of love and friendship.

My mind traveled back to all the parks and woods we explored together. Because of Guylo, my two feet never walked alone. There were always four paws leading the way. I thought of the time I pulled him from the frozen pond. Basically, saving his life. I remembered the car crash where both of us could have easily been killed. All the times he relentlessly chased down softballs with Randy and me. And how could I forget the very first moment I picked him up as a small clumsy puppy.

All of these memories were coming to the forefront of my mind now. I could see him standing on his hind legs reaching the spout of a water fountain drinking the water like he was human. I could almost feel his head resting on my lap while I stroked his head, ears and back. However, the one thing I most assuredly could not see was my life without Guylo.

After what felt like an eternity, the phone rang interrupting my thoughts and prayers. I cautiously picked up the receiver. All I needed to hear was that surgery went well. Guylo is fine and recovering. But I heard the complete opposite. Randy was on the other end. "Guylo didn't make it." Within an instant, those four horrific words destroyed my world.

It was the hardest phone call Randy had ever made. It was the most difficult phone call I ever answered. He was trying to describe what went wrong in surgery. He explained that Guylo's intestines had flipped and too much damage had been done to correct the problem.

At that moment, I heard nothing. All I knew was that Guylo wasn't coming home. I would never again see my angel. Let alone hold him in my arms or stroke his beautiful fur. I fainted. I literally fell with my limp body crashing to the kitchen floor. The receiver falling down beside me. My mom woke up the instant she heard the loud thud of my body hitting the floor. All I can remember is her trying to wake me up. Eventually, I came to. Everything was very fuzzy. But one thing was extremely clear. My beloved Guylo was gone.

Chapter 15.

As Hard As It Is, Life Goes On

Chances are, all of you have been through heartbreak. You've most likely suffered through a tragedy, a death in the family or another type of devastating moment. It's never easy. But, we all find our own way to deal with the pain and sorrow.

My mind was blank, my body numb, and my heart was empty. But, somehow I managed to pull myself together. I had to walk into NBC4 in a matter of hours for my very first day of my new job. It was an unbelievably difficult thing to do. No one knew me nor Guylo. I couldn't talk to anyone about how my entire world had instantly came crashing down.

I could barely breathe. I found it so hard to connect with my new co-workers. But eventually, I made it through the day. When my shift finally came to end, I walked out the back door of the newsroom. I crossed the parking lot motionless and climbed into my car. The same car that Guylo and I rode in together so many times before.

As soon as I shut my driver's side door, the floodgates opened. I sobbed the entire way home. The drive from the TV station to my Westerville home normally takes 20 to 25 minutes. This time, it felt like I was driving in circles for hours. I finally pulled into the driveway and saw Randy's car. I couldn't believe it. He had driven all the way back from Youngstown to help comfort me.

There was no doubt, my heart was completely broken. It was still difficult to breathe or look at anyone without breaking down. I have lived my entire life being a happy, positive, fun-loving, carefree person. Now, I couldn't even crack a smile. Immeasurable sadness had taken over my body, mind and soul.

The other feeling that seemed to consume me was the disgusting feeling of guilt. I will never forgive myself for not being with Guylo as he took his last breath. I've often heard animal experts say that dogs, if they can help it, will not die in front of their owners. They don't want their people to see them suffer or to be sad in anyway. Perhaps, Guylo didn't want me there. Maybe, just maybe, he knew as Randy drove away from my parents' house that evening, that our time together was coming to an end.

But, in my heart, I knew that I had failed him. I wasn't there when he truly needed me to be by his side. It's a sickening feeling. Especially, when Guylo was ALWAYS there for me. Besides, I wasn't at all ready to say goodbye. How could something I loved so strongly be taken from me after such a short time? Guylo and I were together for six short years. However, within that time, I truly learned to love unconditionally. Guylo was, at this point in my life, the closest thing I had to a child. I loved him with every sense of the word, and he loved me right back. We gave each other so much joy, and so many memories that I will forever hold deep within my heart.

Some people can live decades and never experience what Guylo and I shared. I have always believed that you have to make the most of every single day. You really never know when something or someone you so deeply care for will be taken away. I learned that firsthand. We packed so much into those six short years. I am eternally grateful for the time we shared and all those memories that are still so vivid in my mind.

Still today, I often talk to my friends and family about Guylo. I relive all the moments that we created. I try to explain what a powerful bond we formed. Some people seem to understand and empathize with me. Others will truly never understand. It's often through tears that I describe the greatest dog that ever lived.

Over time, I have come to the realization that Guylo really was my guardian angel. There is no other way to look at it. God sent me Guylo for protection, to look after me and keep me from being alone. It's scary moving away from home for the very first time. I never seemed to mind though. I had Guylo. He was right by my side through absolutely everything.

When God brought me home to Central Ohio for my new job at NBC and to be reunited with my family and friends, he took Guylo back. His job was done. In the beginning of this book, I talked about how German Shepherds need jobs. It turns out, Guylo had the most important job of all...to bring me home. I never would have imagined that beginning my dream job would mean the end of Guylo. The Lord giveth, the Lord taketh away.

The End

EPILOGUE

I personally would like to thank you for reading "Guylo". Hopefully, it brought back memories you shared with your own dogs. It also helps to know that we are never alone in grief. There has always been someone who has suffered a loss before us and there will be plenty to suffer after our own personal battles.

I started writing this book 25 years after Guylo and I met, and I held him in my arms for the very first time. I am now married to Randy and we have two wonderful children. Our son Kylan was born in 2001 and our daughter Kamryn was born in 2002. We also have four dogs (Hoops, LC, Whopper and Nick). Two are German Shepherds. We are big believers in rescuing dogs from shelters, pounds or other situations.

When Guylo first passed away, I wasn't sure if I could have another dog, let alone another German Shepherd. I thought it would be too painful and bring back too many memories. Plus, I never wanted Guylo to think that I replaced him. I was wrong.

Randy was the one who pushed me toward getting another dog. His plan was to get a German Shepherd puppy and wrap my engagement ring around its neck with a ribbon. Again, remember what I said about "plans?" He had picked out a puppy from the same place where Guylo came from, but the engagement ring wasn't yet ready from the jeweler. Randy had no choice but to give me the puppy without the ring.

Randy walked into the house one day carrying an adorable German Shepherd pup and handed it to me. I took one look and told Randy that he was taking such a big chance by doing that. But, it didn't take long for my heart to melt. The puppy's name was obvious, "Chance". By the way, Randy and I got engaged a few weeks later.

In total, I have had six dogs since Guylo, including the four current ones. They have all lived long and happy lives. I can't help but wonder where they would have ended up if we didn't give them our home and our hearts.

The hardest part about loving is losing. But, we have to be strong enough to overcome. When something or someone who we so deeply love dies, we cannot be afraid to love again. There are too many unwanted and uncared for animals in this world that suffer in silence. If we don't take them in, who will?

I have loved every one of my pets so much. Each one is different, with their own personalities and characteristics. I will live the rest of my life with dogs. My home would be so empty otherwise. I have had several dogs since my very first one and will continue to have many more. However, there will only be one Guylo. My very first love of my life. Guylo will be in my heart forever.

Mindy Drayer was a TV news anchor/reporter for nearly 25 years before she started co-hosting the talk show "What Matters With Mindy & Mikaela" on iHeartRadio in Columbus, Ohio.

Mindy was born in Minneapolis, Minnesota in 1968 but has lived in Westerville, Ohio for most of her life. In fact, she currently resides in Westerville with her husband Randy, son Kylan and daughter Kami.

Since her beloved Guylo, Mindy has welcomed Chance, Darby, Nick, Whopper, Hoops and L.C. into her family. Dogs will always be a major part of her life.

Mindy spends a great deal of time watching her kids play travel and high school sports and rooting on the Hartley Hawks where her husband is the Head Varsity Boys Basketball Coach. She also enjoys exercising and socializing with friends and family. She is a strong opponent against animal abuse and cruelty of any kind.

You can follow Mindy on:
Facebook (Mindy Drayer Public Figure)
Twitter (mdrayer1)
Instagram (drayermindy)

You can also tune into What Matters With Mindy & Mikaela Sundays from 4-6pm. Listen online at www.610wtvn.com